About the Author

Iain Manson was born and raised in the Craigentinny area of Edinburgh, and attended the city's Royal High School. Upon leaving school in the late 60s, he enrolled at Agricultural College, and after a mixture of practical and theoretical studies, he qualified with a diploma in Farm Business Management. After a couple of positions within the industry, Iain opted for a career change that would enable him to progress for better promotion and financial opportunities. So, he took a position in the grocer, confectioner and tobacco trade working for a couple of national wholesalers, specializing on Business Development and Key Account Selling. Iain was having a wonderful career until that moment on 14th January 1993 when his life changed forever.

Dedication

I dedicate this book to the entire orthopaedic surgical team, doctors, nurses and my physios at Ward 26 in the old Royal Infirmary of Edinburgh and the Princess Margaret Rose Hospital, without whose care and expertise, I would not be here today.

Also, to all my good friends and crew working with P&O cruises who have played a major role in my life over the last five years.

Not forgetting my faithful companion Maxie boy, the Yorkie that helped me keep my focus and positivity for ten years until the wee man passed away in 2006.

Lastly, the Physio's at The Princess Margaret Rose Hospital in Edinburgh and to the Fire and Rescue crew at Kelso Fire Station.

Iain Manson

FROM CRASH TO CASH, CARAVANS AND CRUISES

A brief Painful but Humorous
Journey of a Survivor

AUSTIN MACAULEY PUBLISHERS™
LONDON • CAMBRIDGE • NEW YORK • SHARJAH

Copyright © Iain Manson 2024

The right of Iain Manson to be identified as author of this work has been asserted by the author in accordance with sections 77 and 78 of the Copyright, Designs and Patents Act 1988.

All rights reserved. No part of this publication may be reproduced, stored in a retrieval system, or transmitted in any form or by any means, electronic, mechanical, photocopying, recording, or otherwise, without the prior permission of the publishers.

Any person who commits any unauthorised act in relation to this publication may be liable to criminal prosecution and civil claims for damages.

All of the events in this memoir are true to the best of author's memory. The views expressed in this memoir are solely those of the author.

A CIP catalogue record for this title is available from the British Library.

ISBN 9781035805389 (Paperback)
ISBN 9781035805396 (ePub e-book)

www.austinmacauley.com

First Published 2024
Austin Macauley Publishers Ltd®
1 Canada Square
Canary Wharf
London
E14 5AA

Acknowledgements

A very special thanks goes to SCID (Scottish Campaign against Irresponsible Drivers) and Paul Flynn (MP). Their continued support and lobbying for the removal of bull bars was much appreciated.

Also, a very special acknowledgement to my trusted and special friend Smitha Kurup for her valued time spent on formatting and illustrating this book.

Finally, Smitha Kurup is credited with the cover design and book.

Chapter One
I Really Shouldn't Be Here

Later that day, the same Fire Engine collided with a bridge parapet that straddles the River Tweed resulting in one of the firemen losing his life, so, as you can imagine, it was extremely hard for me to comprehend that earlier that same day he had played a major role in helping save my life only later to lose his. Life can indeed be so cruel.

Family and friends who visited me early on told me that I was unrecognisable, that my head was the size of a beach ball and that I had more tubes sticking out of me than an irrigation plant. My family was told to prepare for the worst and that I had a brain bleed, whereby they had to drill into my skull and insert drain straws. The next 48 hours would be crucial, then the weird and the wonderful dreaming began. I was aware of something going on, but it was hard to explain as there were distant voices and the strange feeling of being moved, etc. The dreams were intense. The first I remember about being awake was a suction machine and the noise of a nurse holding a tube in my throat.

My parents and the sales director of the company I worked for were all standing over me at this point. I had no idea what was going on or, indeed, what had happened. They told me that I had been in a very serious car crash and I was lucky to be alive. They explained the severity of my injuries, which I will go into detail later.

It was at this point that my immediate thoughts turned to my little dog, a purebred blue and tan Yorkshire Terrier called Max. He was our world and used to accompany me everywhere, remaining in my car while I called on my various customers. He got his fair share of 'walkies' in between my calls and seemed to enjoy his life in the car.

Obviously, the first thing that came into my now conscious mind was the realisation that he must have been killed, so when my wife at the time told me that although I survived the crash, there was still bad news, so understandably, upon hearing this, I immediately said to her, "It's Maxie boy; he didn't make it?"

"No, no," she said. The accident had happened on a Thursday, her day off, and Max was home with her.

"Wow, great!" I said. "So what's the bad news then? Was the crash my fault?"

"No, no," was the reply again. The other driver had apparently pleaded guilty to careless driving and had been charged. She then broke down in tears and said, "It's your right eye, Iain; they could not save it."

"Oh!" I said. "Is that all?" At this point and with that comment, the doctors knew I was going to be a fighter. Bull Bars tore my life apart; now I want to smash them! It took a few years but with the help of now deceased Labour MP, Paul Flynn we did indeed smash them thanks to his Bill which he managed to steer successfully through Parliament via the support of SCAID (Scottish Campaign Against Irrespnsible Drivers).

First night in the main orthopaedic ward, I tried to turn onto my side but fell out of the bed and onto the hard floor with blood pouring from my nose. It was at this point that all the emotions and reality checks kicked in, and I completely broke down and sobbed my heart out. Two of the ward nurses, who ultimately became good friends, showed concern and complete understanding and were first-class in listening to all my concerns and anxieties, etc. For the next couple of weeks, the visitors came and went like waves in the ocean, and their kindness and good wishes were real blessings. The unfortunate thing, however, was that I could not speak to them as my jaws were wired together in order to fix and heal all the various facial fractures. This is where I had to adopt the art of sign language and scribbling on pieces of paper, but it did the trick.

After a couple of days of getting acclimatised in the main ward, in walks this girl, wearing a white tunic and blue slacks. She introduces herself as my physio and proceeds to assemble a form of scaffolding around my bed. This takes her a good couple of hours, and then in her South African accent, she proceeds to inform me that this is the structure that is going to be your best friend, Iain, and that it would aid my recovery whilst I was bedridden. OMG! The journey was about to begin.

Chapter Two
Life Will Never Be
the Same Again

So, the physio started with a strict programme that I must adhere to. This will be covered in later chapters.

It was a Monday morning about six weeks into my stay in the hospital, and the consultants and doctors were undertaking their morning ritual of ward rounds. I distinctly remember my registrar leaning forward over my bed and uttering these words: "You must come to terms now that the old Iain Manson is gone."

Well, talk about telling it how it is and not pulling any punches. Those few words really hit home, and when an expert tells them to you, then you really start to believe them. I certainly took it to board, and at that point, I think it was the moment I realised and believed that I had a very long journey ahead of me with many limitations. I was told by my physio that unless I undertook three hours of physiotherapy three days a week for one full year, I would spend the rest of my life in a wheelchair.

Well, for me, that was a 'no-brainer', especially as I was so focussed and passionate about getting back behind the wheel of a car again, as I knew for sure now that driving would play a major role in my future mobility. I was informed that I would need to take a special driving course to determine my suitability and capability and if I could, in fact, continue to drive a manual-operated gearbox or if an automatic might be the only option. That did not sit well with me as I needed to feel in control. This was a residual physiological feeling after the accident, but it sure did give me the impetus and incentive to put everything into my recovery programme. The severity of the destruction of my legs was made clear to me one day while I was sitting waiting for the patient transport ambulance outside the orthopaedic hospital.

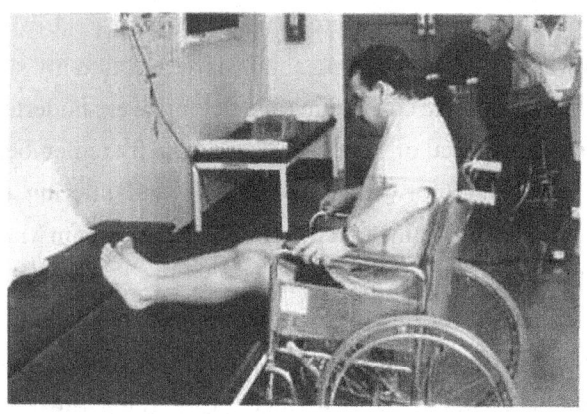

When I got a tap on my shoulder, the voice said to me, "Hello there. Nice to see you sitting already. You will not remember me, but I was the surgeon in your consultant's team who had the task of removing the smashed kneecaps with the vacuum suction machines." He went on to say, "Your kneecaps were like broken teeth, and I can honestly tell you that if you had these injuries ten years ago, then for sure you would have lost your right leg and possibly the left one." My god, another reality check and as to the extent of my injuries, but this was only to be the beginning.

As part of the process of my settlement claim against the other driver, a series of physical and physiological tests had to be undertaken as to the complete extent of my injuries. This would take nearly two and a half years and ultimately highlight in full all of what has happened.

Chapter Three
Hospital Life

So, my physio completed the scaffolding apparatus around my bed and gave me specific upper body exercises for approximately one hour per day, but with me being a determined 'sod' and hell-bent on impressing her with my progress, I did my hour through the day but also a further couple of hours in the middle of the night while the rest of the ward was asleep.

After a couple of weeks, I got to know the purpose of this newfound upper body strength: it was to gain enough strength in my arms for what lay ahead. Yip! The enemy: the wheelchair.

Every day, like clockwork, she would come for me one hour before lunch and push me down to the gym, where I was mainly doing hand and eye coordination exercises and sitting up balancing, etc. Remember, at this stage, I had two badly smashed upper legs that were being held together with an assortment of pins, plates and wire mesh, one eye, a cheekbone and two jaws that resembled a jigsaw. There was also a wall of titanium plates that ran the full length of my forehead, including my eye sockets. So, in total, I was told that I had approximately forty pins, plates, etc. in my body.

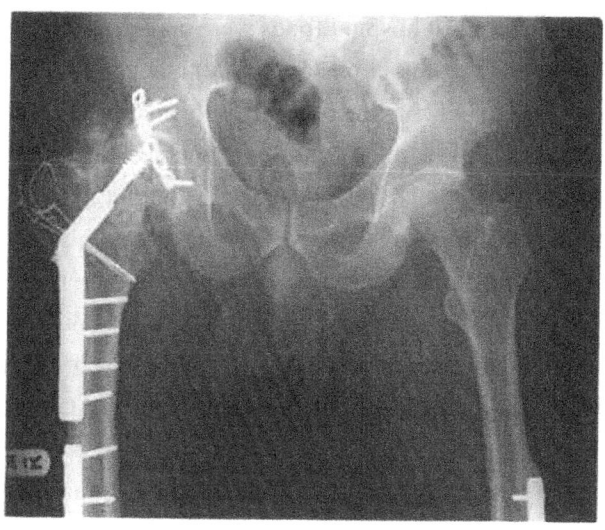

So, it was back to the ward for my food supplement drink to be injected into my abdominal feed tube. Wow! The luxury of it all. My sense of taste and smell were well gone due to the sub-cranial nerve being severed, and if that was not enough, the nerve damage had caused complete numbness along the right-hand side of my chin and bottom lip.

I was to find out later, once I started eating again, that whenever I had finished, I needed to sneeze. This was due to the mixed messages coming from my brain to the damaged facial nerve network. By this time, my wife then had been a constant companion to me, and as a nurse herself, she had left her job so she could care for me full-time upon my eventual discharge from the hospital. She would come to the hospital for lunchtime to help the nurses with their meal duties, etc. and stay with me until the end of the afternoon visiting. Although I still could not sample the food at this stage, I have to say that it looked rather appealing considering the reputation that most hospital foods were tagged with.

I distinctly remember one of the staff nurses sitting on the end of my bed and chatting with my wife and myself, saying that statistics show that the majority of couples that have been through the same degree of trauma as us do not make it and end up separating, so she emphasised that we both must stay strong and positive. Well, we sure did, and we remained married for 26 years. As a parting footnote to this discussion, the staff nurse gave myself and my wife a very serious potential to contemplate, as she said off the record that it was probably just as well that I did not carry an organ donor card, as because of the critical life-threatening injury that I sustained and because of my relatively young age, a spur-of-the-moment decision not to necessarily resuscitate me may have been a favourable option. Therefore, in these circumstances, a certain organ removable from a non-deceased person might have seemed quite a favourable road to go down. So, needless to say, I have never carried a donor card since.

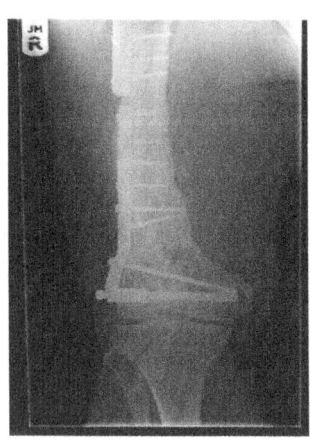

So now that I have mastered the wheelchair, I am pushing myself down to the gym and back to the ward, basically killing time, until I get my leg plasters and braces removed and start the long and arduous task of learning to walk again.

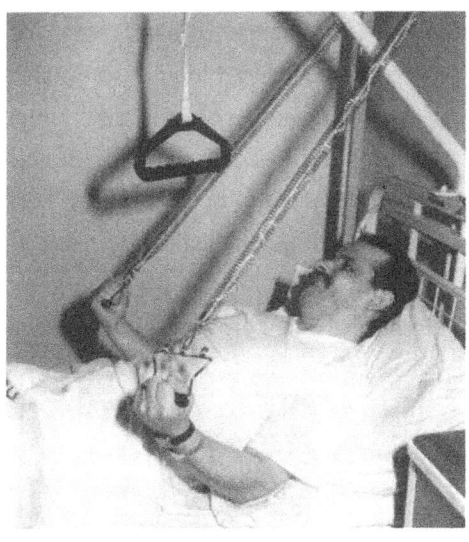

Before the use of the commode whilst using the wheelchair, my toilet needs (whilst bedridden) were accommodated by the infamous bedpan. It is a very true saying that at this point one's vanity goes out the window, but there is no choice in the matter and needs must, as they say. However, all the nursing staff, apart from one, were excellent with me when it came to supply and demand, if you know what I mean. The 'one' I am referring to was a right-stuck-up 'youse'. I am being very polite calling her that! She hated the thought of you daring to request the need to relieve yourself just prior to mealtimes. You got the impression from the silly woman that you were expected to adhere to certain suitable times, etc. Talk about a little Hitler! She knew all right that I had her sussed, and she didn't like that. Me and her never got on, and I believe she is now a watchmaker in Switzerland!

Due to the mass of painkillers, etc. that I was taking, this has the profound effect of giving you serious constipation. This is common knowledge. Now, most patients can overcome this with the use of liquid solutions or indeed suppositories. But oh, no! Not me. My pipework was completely and totally blocked so that only thing left for me was the dreaded 'Fairy liquid' bottle right up the you know what! The enema to give its medical name.

Image of the knife-wielding maniac in the movie *Psycho*, then that is more or less the persona of this individual.

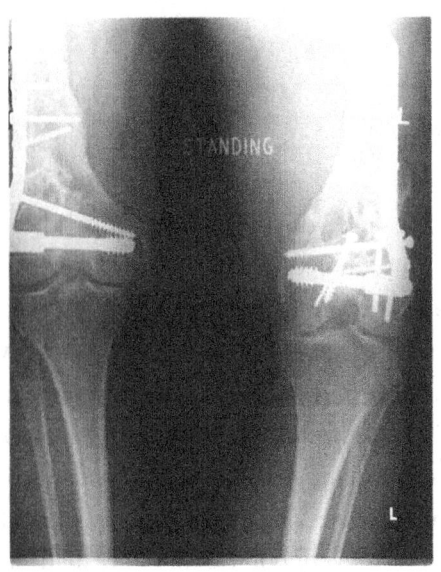

So, the hilarious crescendo happened when, finally, Mr Psycho heard the mutterings of Mr Homeless and wee 'Jimmy'. Well, Mr Psycho could take no more and proceeded to go over to Mr Homeless's bed, lean over him and utter the words, "Av just killed wee Jimmy, so he is effing dead, so will you now shut the F—K up?" So now Mr Homeless started crying, and the nurses came over to see what all the fuss was about. Mr Psycho proceeded to tell them that he had just cut wee Jimmy's throat, and at this point, he is smartly escorted back to his bed. 'Talk About One Flew Over the Cuckoo's Nest'.

Now I feel the time is right to pay a visit and thank the intensive care nursing staff, who, together with the surgeons, worked so hard to save my life. After thanking one of the senior staff nurses, he proceeded to inform me that fourth eight hours, they knew for sure that I would pull through. He said that they knew I was a fighter, and he went on to tell me that when I was waking from my coma, I tried to get out of my bed and when one of the nurses tried to settle me, I duly tried to punch her in the face. It's amazing what strong medication can make you do. Thank God, they saw the funny side of it, but I still felt somewhat ashamed and embarrassed. Then, as if that was not bad enough, apparently, I had demanded an HIV test, as for some reason, I got it into my head that the hospital had been supplying me with prostitutes. How am I going to live this down!

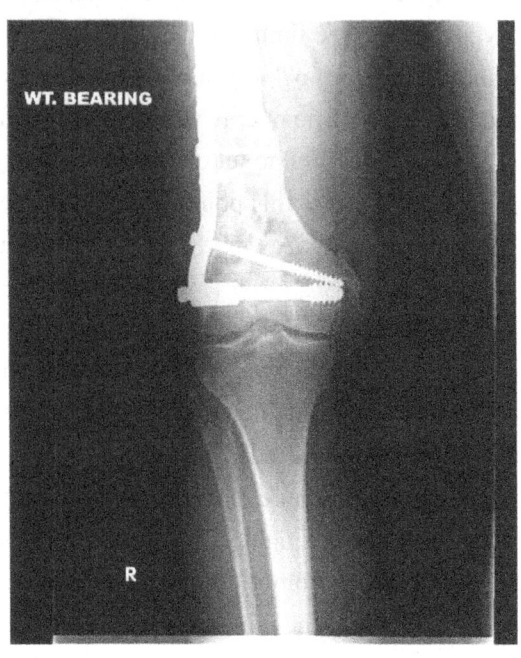

One day, in the main ward, while on my bed reading the paper, I noticed the name badge – for the first time – of one of the nurses. It read, John Wardhaugh. Well, being the fanatical Jambo that I am, I obviously had to ask him if he had any relation to 'Twinkle Toes', the prolific goal scorer, Jimmy Wardhaugh, a member of the 'Terrible Trio', who terrified and tormented defences in the 1950s and '60s. His reply to me was to wait and see, which I thought was somewhat strange, but nevertheless, I just accepted his answer.

To my thrill and absolute amazement, the next morning again, he came straight over to my bed and pulled this medal out of his staff tunic. He gave it to me and let me read the wording, which said Scottish Cup – Winners 1956. Hold me back! So, it turned out that Jimmy Wardhaugh was John's father, and the cup winners medal was to commemorate Hearts' 3–1 victory over Celtic. Well, as you can imagine, that made my day.

At this time, there was a male cardiology student in the ward, and we became good friends. He was the type of guy to whom you could ask anything and he would give you a straight answer. I used to pester a lot by asking why the surgeons and many of the doctors would not dwell on telling you the risks and negatives of various operations and procedures, etc. He explained that a positive mindset was crucial to aid recovery, maintain a focus, etc. He also stressed to me that I try to get out of the hospital as soon as possible because there can be a hive of infection, etc., and the longer one is in there, then obviously, the greater the risk. These words were to prove so true, which I will explain in a later chapter. While in the process of chatting about my accident, he quoted some mind-blowing statistics to me. He said that in a funny, peculiar kind of way that maybe it was fate that I suffered but survived the crash because if I had carried on with my lifestyle that consisted of smoking, drinking and filling with lunchtime pies and chips, etc., then there was a very real chance that I would not see my fifty. Wow! A REAL WAKE-UP CALL straight from the horse's mouth, so to speak. Maybe I do have a guardian angel!

Chapter Four
No Pain, No Gain

The long and winding road to recovery
Like I mentioned earlier, I was smoking approximately thirty cigarettes a day and was somewhat overweight, so there was a definite potential risk to me during the eighteen hours of invasive surgery while the team was using all their expertise to basically rebuild me. However, this was trauma-based surgery and not elective, so there was no choice in the matter. While in my coma, I contracted pneumonia in the right lung; apparently, this can be quite a common complaint due to my circumstances. The doctors decided that I needed the lung drained of the infected fluid and the other content. The other contents, in fact, consisted of a thick black liquid tar-like solution, and my wife was then asked if they should keep this content to show me my recovery in the hope that it would put a stop to my smoking for good.

Well, least said, this was a no-brainer, and I suppose this decision was also made easier for me by the fact that I actually felt no further cravings again any way. NOT the easiest or preferred method to stop smoking, but it sure as hell worked for me. In one of the beds opposite me, I had noticed a young Asian guy who always seemed to be sleeping and did not appear to be communicating at all with the nursing staff, and that included my physio. I asked her what the problem was, and she said that he had been knocked off his motorbike and had a severely broken leg and needed a much more positive attitude if he was to make a complete recovery. However, she felt that whatever the reason he had just switched off. She asked if I would like to feel myself over, cry and engage some sort of chat with him and highlight the extent of the recovery that I have made so far. Oh well, sad to say that my muttering fell on deaf ears, and I heard on my return as an outpatient to one of my clinics that he needed his leg amputated.

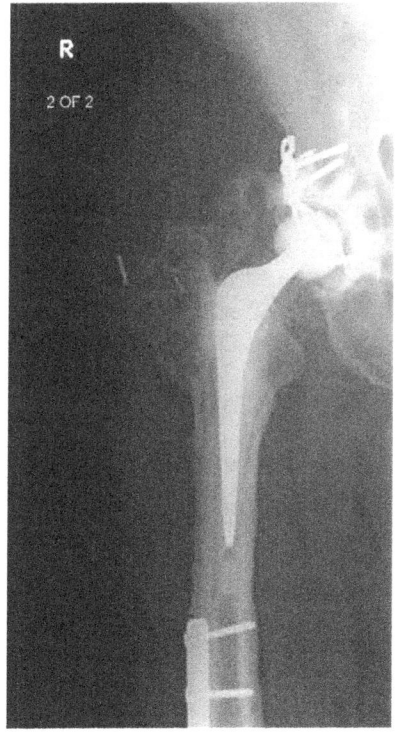

A very definitive reminder of the term from the physiotherapy bible: no pain, no gain. After days of bed and gym leg exercises, there proved to be quite a serious problem with me gaining even ninety-degree flexion in my right knee joint. Although the right leg was the more severely smashed of the two, I should have been, by now, gaining more bend through the joint. This became very frustrating for me, as it was definitely slowing my recovery and my ability to walk again. It felt like there was a tight elastic band over the joint, making it feel extremely stiff.

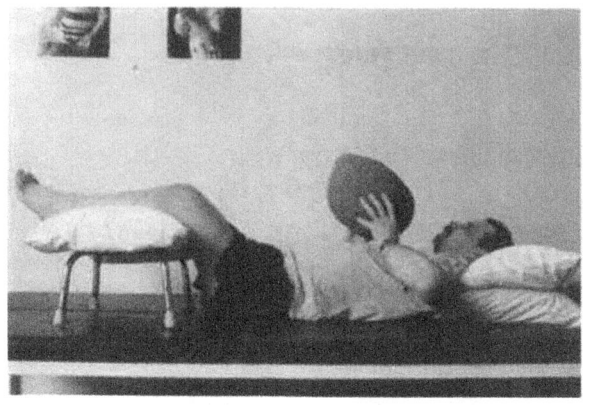

After I was showing some concern regarding the prognosis for this, one of the most senior orthopaedic surgeons came to see me and informed me that when people have the area of brain injury that I have, it can have a similar effect that a stroke sufferer can endure. He said, however, that most stroke sufferers do not have a mangled upper leg at the same time, and there has been a band of muscle forming over the joint as a part of the body's healing process. He explained that this complication mainly arose on the right leg, again similar to a stroke victim suffering damage primarily down the one side. A decision was reached whereby a piece of apparatus called a knee mobiliser would be hooked up to me.

It would be set at various degrees of flexion, and it was hoped that after three days there should be significant improvement. So, the plan was that this electrically operated device would quietly move my knee joint to and fro throughout the night while I attempted to get some sleep. There would be a rest period for breakfast, lunch and visiting, but that was it. My determination got me through, however, with the realistic thought for a positive outcome. How wrong I was!

If there was any improvement, it was immeasurable, so it was decided that a procedure called a quadricepsplasty would be undertaken, whereby they would cut the restrictive band of muscle in the hope that this may help, but it was stressed to me that because this condition was neurological and not physical, it may not work. This was my only hope, so the operation was scheduled over the ensuing couple of days. I felt quite apprehensive at this point, as this would be the first surgical procedure that I would be aware of.

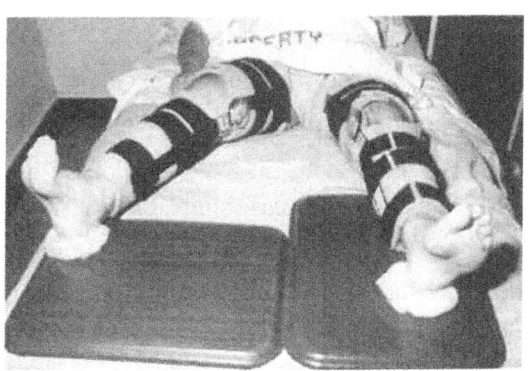

So, the moment arose, and I am to be first on the operation list. Duly suited, booted and informed of the usual risks, etc., I am wheeled down to the theatre, where I am met in the pre-op room by the anaesthetist, a larger-than-life character who, while trying to keep me calm, informs me he is a Hibernian supporter. "Well," I say, "I have to tell you that I am a fanatical Jambo (Hearts supporter), so no funny stuff or overdoses, thank you very much." We both have a good laugh, and his reassurance to me is first-class. So, he starts to get some colour on my cheeks by giving me some oxygen, then asks me to count to five. One, two, three, four, five...Game over. I am out cold!

I woke up in recovery, and I am glad to be alive. I am on a self-controlled morphine trigger for pain relief, and beside the two draining tubes that are extending from my thigh and groin, I am amazed to see that the knee mobiliser is back doing its stuff. I am told that it is imperative that I keep it going for as long as I can, although this time the pain was really severe. So, I am given constant painkillers to dull it because I simply must endure it if I have any chance of a positive outcome. Like I mentioned earlier, if there is progress to be made, then I am your man.

A few days later, my physio appears and is pleased with my progress. She informs me that my consultant is hosting a European seminar of orthopaedic surgeons at the PMR research centre's lecture theatre and they would like me to attend as he wants me as his case study. Obviously, I agree to this, and the necessary arrangements are made for me to be transferred there for an overnight stay. The consultants arrive at my bedside to inform me that there is no time to be wheeled in in person, then he tells me that he will be discussing all my injuries, x-rays and operations as part of his talk. I agree to this, and he leaves by saying that he will see me the next day.

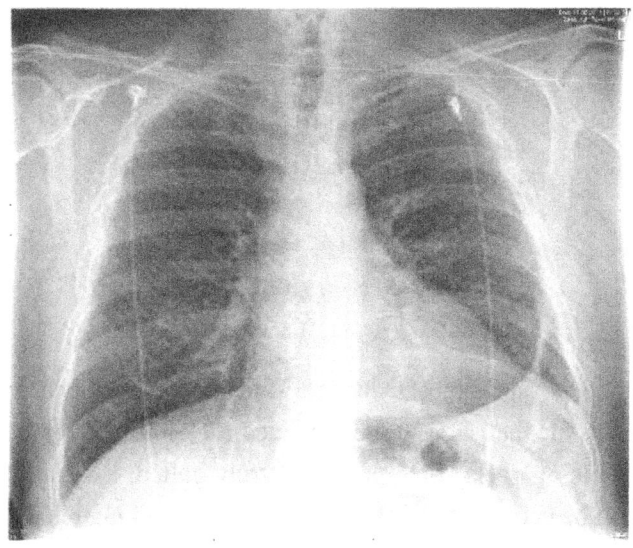

Now is the moment the screen is pulled around my bed and two nurses close themselves in with me. "What is happening?" I asked.

"It's your lucky day," came the reply. "We are going to remove your drain tube."

"OH, is that all?" I said. Now this may hurt a bit, so on the count of three, I had to take an almighty deep breath. "Oh my god!" I let out a yell that must have sounded like a frustrated cat.

"Well done, Iain," they said. "That's it. Done." Here we go again – no pain, no gain!

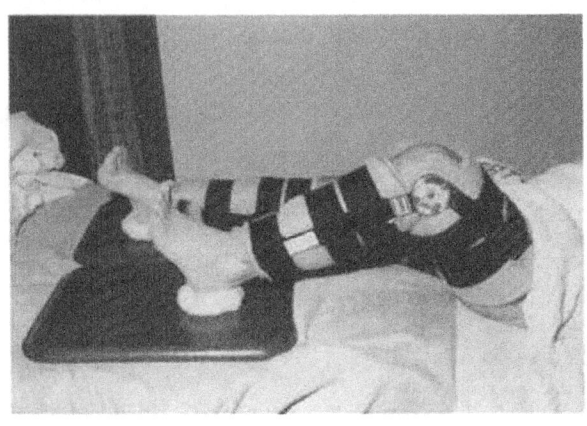

My physio appears about a couple of hours later and informs me that she is to be seconded back to Cape Town for a couple of weeks' time, and I am truly gutted. I wanted her to still be here so she could be a part of my walking rehab. So sad! I proceeded to say to her, "Oh well, then, if you get me walking again before you go, then I'll buy you the biggest box of chocolate I can get." She looks at me, smiles and thanks me for the kind gesture, but says in a very matter-of-fact tone that although she is good and I am so positive, she is not a magician. That was the reality check I did not want to hear, but she had to be honest with me. I tell her that a box of chocolates will be waiting for her if and when she ever returns.

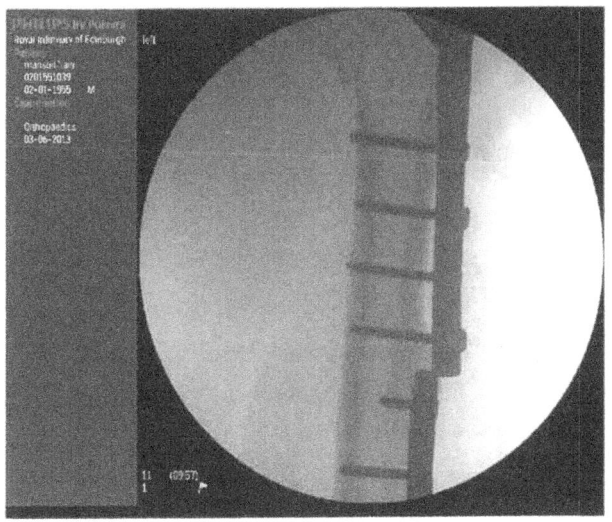

After a further day or so, I start to cough up blood, and everyone's suspicions of a clot seem to be proving correct. However, to my delight, the next day, the scan results are available, and the charge nurse comes to my bedside to inform me that I have pleurisy. So, I am immediately hooked up to an antibiotics drip and told that I must discharge the phlegm that my now-constant coughing is producing into a sputum dish. Pleurisy is extremely painful when taking in a breath and coughing, and it can scar the lung tissue for life. However, after about a week, the antibiotics seem to have worked, and I am feeling much better.

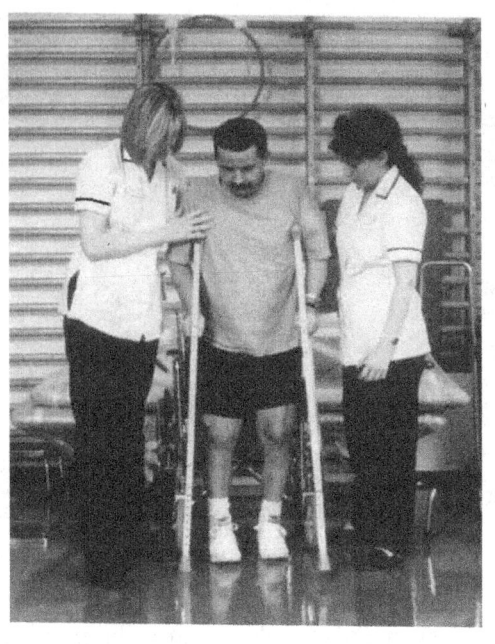

I start to develop a very sensitive soreness on the inside of my left knee. What bloody next? I ask myself. So next morning, during their rounds, I inform my surgeon of this. He looks at my knee and presses it upon, whereby I just about jumped out of the bed, and he told me he could feel an abnormality and told me he would put me down for an exploratory operation the next day. By now, thankfully, I am finished with the knee mobiliser, and they seem quite pleased. All things considered, I now have about a sixty-degree flexion, acceptable at this stage, but much more intense physio awaits. The plan is that it will all start in a big style after my operation on the other knee.

So now I am getting prepared for only the second operation that I am going to be conscious of. They tell me that it should last about an hour and a half. So obviously somewhat less than the quadricepsplasty and quite minuscule compared to my overall operations, which presently stand at eleven or twelve. But I can tell that operations and needles are something that I could never get used to.

Oh well, here we go again. The porters arrive to take me down to my second home: the operating theatre, where I have a date with Mr Hibby, the anaesthetist. Sure as fate, there he is waiting for me with a smile the length of Leith Walk on his face, and I am sure I can read his lips. Now another sad Jambo goes under the knife yet again.

I wake up in recovery, and my surgeon tells me that they had to file down a bone spike. This stems from bone callouses that can form as new bone generates under the body's healing process. I am now wondering why the anaesthetist makes a point of coming into the recovery room with a massive smile on his face as he tells me to enjoy my day. I am thinking, strange! But all becomes very clear to me as I enter the ward and go into shock and a complete meltdown when all around my bed area and on the wall above my bed are plastered a multitude of green and white ribbons and balloons, not to mention a foil cut out of the Scottish Cup and a banner that read, 'Hardlines, Iain, but Hibs have just won the Scottish Cup'. So, through my somewhat recovery haze, I started to believe that this had actually happened. Talk about being stitched up, literally! I it got to handed to me though, he had the entire ward staff and patients in on it. What a laugh!

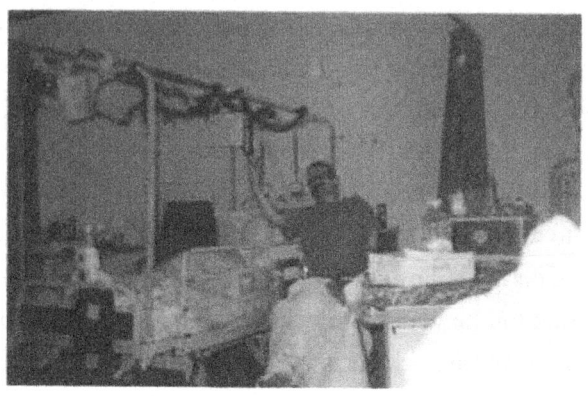

Now that my eye socket has healed and returned to its normal orbital expanse, it's time to start the glass-eye fittings, or to give it its medical term, ocular prothesis. So this larger-than-life 'Geordie' woman bounces up to the side of my bed and introduces herself as the glass eye technician. Posh name for a 'fitter'. "Sorry that you have had to wait for a while, 'Pet'," she says, "but we have to be sure that everything is healed so we can proceed with the correct size of your prosthetic eye." She spends about thirty minutes explaining all the bathing procedures and self-fitting methods before inserting what she believes is a very good match. I tell her that I will crack the jokes, thank you very much, as it is no more a match than flying in the air. She tells me not to worry and that it will be just a temporary one, as there is still a little bit of swelling that needs to be reduced yet. So, I am literally now in the same world as the preverbal National Health Spectacle, and we all know about them.

My mind is already made up by now that to get any decent match, I have to go private. Anyway, I humour her on her subsequent visits and tell her that 'I am as happy as Larry'. She seems delighted that I am so pleased.

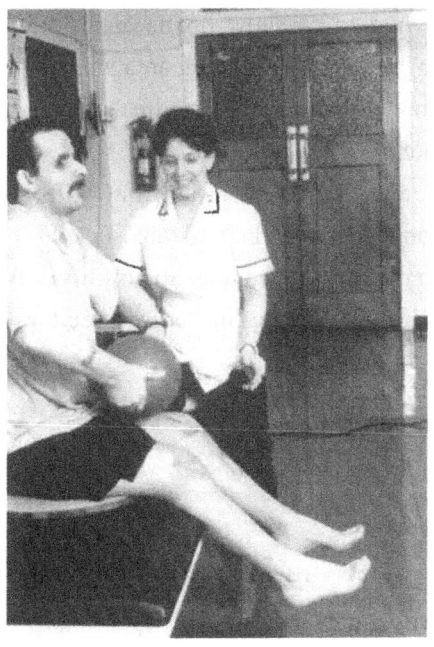

One of the first things that I do once I start driving again is to make an appointment at Canniesburn Hospital on the outskirts of Glasgow to discuss all the future options and possibilities regarding further surgery and a decent-looking prosthesis. I am informed that there is a first-class prosthetic technician who works privately out of Perth Royal Infirmary. So I duly make an appointment to meet with him. In the meantime, the specialist at Canniesburn Hospital tells me that there is an ophthalmic surgeon at the Western Infirmary in Glasgow who specialises in coral implants, whereby a 'peg' is attached to the back of the glass eye and the peg itself is attached to a piece of coral, which is sutured into the muscle that controls movement behind the eye. The purpose was that once in place, you could actually move the glass eye within the eye socket. My first port of call therefore was to the Western Infirmary in Glasgow, but because the loss of my eye and the damage to the surrounding area was caused by severe trauma and not by any type of medical condition, etc., they had their doubts if it would therefore be a success. In any event, they gave it their best shot, but unfortunately, they found too much damage behind the socket, so they were unable to carry out this technique. So now my only option was to arrange a visit to the guy in Perth to see how realistic he could make my prosthesis.

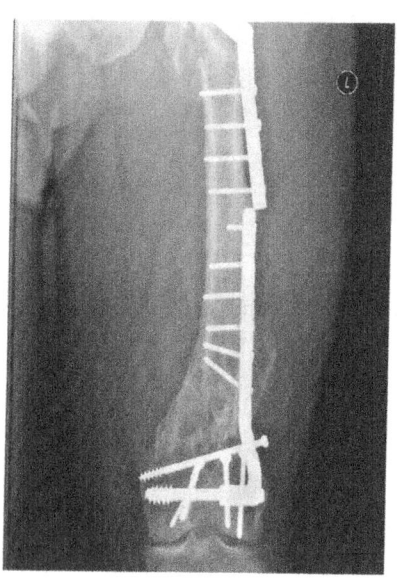

After my first appointment in Perth, I witnessed enough examples of this expert's work to fill me with confidence for what lay ahead, and after my six visits over an eight-month period to get the finished article fitted, I was deliriously happy. My prosthesis was hand-painted and glazed to perfection. He explained to me that it would last a lifetime and could withstand being driven over without sustaining any damage.

To this day, people just think that I have a damaged and droopy eyelid, and I can also give proof and testament to this because during the time I went to my optician for my very first eye test, I wanted to play a joke on the optician and say nothing about me only having one eye. Well, talk about having a laugh! She checks my left eye first with the ophthalmoscope and then asks me to open the right one, to which I oblige. "Oh," she says, "you never told me that you wore a prosthetic eye."

Ha-ha! I say, "You never asked."

"Well, it's extremely realistic," she said, "and it did fool me for a second or so." That's all I needed to hear to prove to me that my man in Perth had provided me with the 'Real McCoy'.

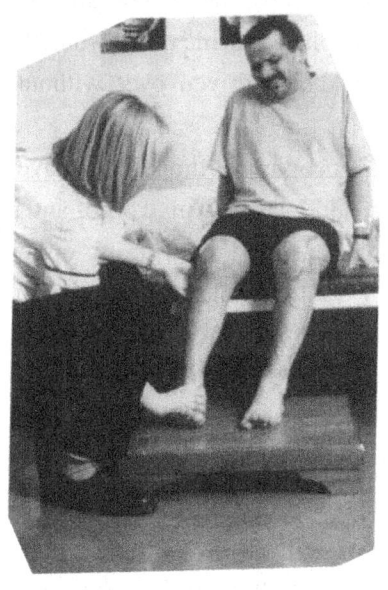

So, to carry on the theme of having a laugh, by far the best one was one night when lying in my bed, two of the ward nurses came over to me and, knowing that I was up for a laugh, asked me if I would help them play a joke on a new junior doctor who was on duty this very night. One of the girls had three or four green furry toy frogs that she produced from a carrier bag, and they wanted me to inform this doctor that I had symptoms that felt like I had a frog in my throat, whereby I was then to open my pyjama's top and this frog would fall out. Sounded perfect to me, so the scene was set. I was to do one better than that and ask them to give me all the frogs, which I secured around my throat area with a towel. The nurses then sprinkled droplets of water on my forehead to make it look like sweat. So, they now paged the junior doctor to inform him that one of the long-term patients on the ward was feeling somewhat unwell and would he come and examine me. After about 15 minutes, this baby-faced doctor arrives at my bed and asks me what seems to be the problem. I tell him that I am feeling hot. He takes my temperature, and it is normal. I then inform him that I have a bit of a croak, and that it feels like I have a frog in my throat.

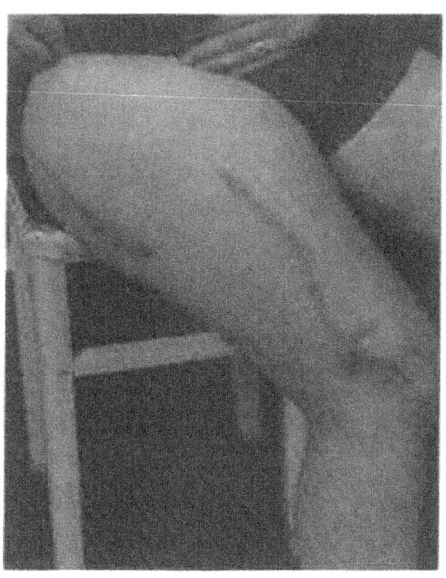

Struggling by this time to keep a straight face and hear a couple of giggling nurses in the background, he proceeds to sound my chest with the stethoscope, but just before he does, I can no longer hold back my laughter and quickly say to him that it doesn't just feel like I have one frog in my throat but a whole family of them as I undo the towel from around my neck and they all fall out onto my chest. Well, to say he was not amused is an understatement. He replaces his stethoscope, stamps his feet and marches away. The nurses told me the next day that they got a 'ticking off', but it was all well worth it. Hear! Hear!

Today, I am waiting for the transport ambulance to take me to the maxillofacial department at the City Hospital to have the wires removed from my jaws. I have had them in for seven weeks now, so really only one week behind the six-week norm for such an injury. I am full of optimism now that I know my feed tube to my stomach will soon be history. I am met in the treatment room with two nurses, who proceed to give six local anaesthetic injections all the way around my jawline. Some fifteen minutes later, they snip one end of the jaw wire that has been protruding through my face and now proceed to clamp the other knotted end with surgical pliers and tell me that they will pull the wire all the way through my jawbone and that I will feel a strange sensation. Now comes the proverbial nurse's war cry of 'take a deep breath', to which I obey. Oh, my bloody god! The pain is unbearable, and I am screaming like a 'banshee'. It's over with after a few seconds, but to me, it feels like ages. The anaesthetic obviously has not done its job, and I have never ever experienced pain like this. One of the nurses says, "Well done, Iain; you are one of the few people who can now brag about the fact that you have experienced pain worse than that of childbirth." If that was meant to be a comfort for me, then it sure as hell didn't work, and I asked to be returned to the Royal Hospital asap. I wasn't a happy chappy.

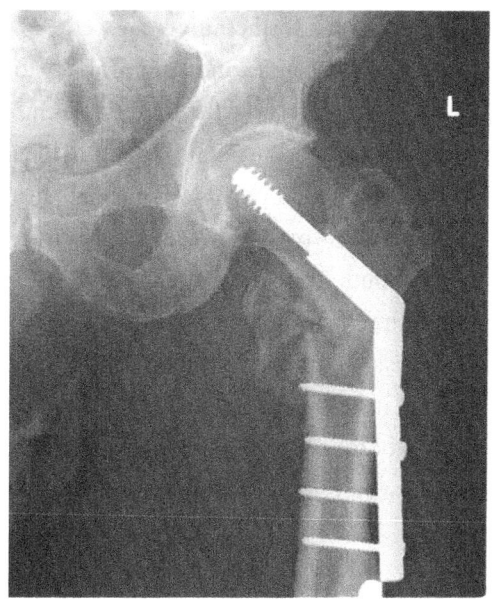

"Not so quick," one of the nurses informs me, "the consultant maxillofacial surgeon who rebuilt your face wants to see you." I find out, at this point, that he is a professor of Swiss nationality and one of the top maxillofacial surgeons in Europe. He also does a lot of private work in London and was responsible for rebuilding the face of Tottenham Hotspur football legend Gary Mabbutt, MBE. I remember his dreadful injury making the news headlines. The Swiss surgeon duly appears and has a good look at his handywork and asks me if I am pleased. I tell him I am, apart from today's experience, and he rightly informs me that it is a small price to pay, all things considered! He says to me that he advises I have a further two operations, one to improve the orbit contour around my eye socket and another to realign and thus make my nose more symmetrical. He asks how I feel about his suggestion, and I commit to the first procedure, and he says he will write to me with a forthcoming date, etc.

Now the ambulance is here, and I am off back to my main ward, and I ask if I can now have the food tube removed from my stomach. This is agreed, and again, I am told to take a deep breath. 'Out it comes with a pop'. Much to my surprise, this was not too painful. Now my physio comes to see me and asks me to open my mouth as wide as I can. Shit! I can't. "Just what I thought," she said. She tells me that I am going to have to do mouth exercises four to six times a day for a month. In the meantime, she informs me that my diet is going to be soup, soup and more bloody soup, followed by a nutritional drink via straw. What I would give for a cheese sandwich!

Chapter Five
The Settlement

A New Life Awaits

At times, this episode in my life seems more stressful than the actual physical trauma of my accident. A family friend's son was a solicitor, and they were keen to take on my case for compensation, obviously. But the amount involved was potentially very significant, to say the least. There was no time to waste, and the process started while I was still in the hospital, the bedside chats, etc. all in the name of information gathering regarding mainly the background to my life, career, hobbies and interests, etc.

Then, once I was home, it seemed that there was not a day that passed without correspondence coming through the letterbox. As there was now no money at all coming into the house and the fact that I was told the case could take up to six years before settlement, it was decided that my solicitor would apply to the Court of Session for an interim payment. This actually was awarded very promptly indeed, much to my surprise. We took this opportunity to go to Cyprus for a well-deserved break and some sunshine. I was not fit for much, but I managed to do some swimming, which had been strongly recommended by the physios. After returning home, there were more requests to attend a medical assessment, both from my solicitor and from the other party's side. It is important to mention at this stage that the guy who nearly killed me was fined one hundred and fifty pounds and had six penalty points placed on his licence. Apparently, the courts took review of the fact that he had no intention of going out that morning to drive his vehicle into anyone and also the fact that at twenty years of age, he could have panicked and left me to perish at the side of the road but instead had gone to a local farm and raised the alarm.

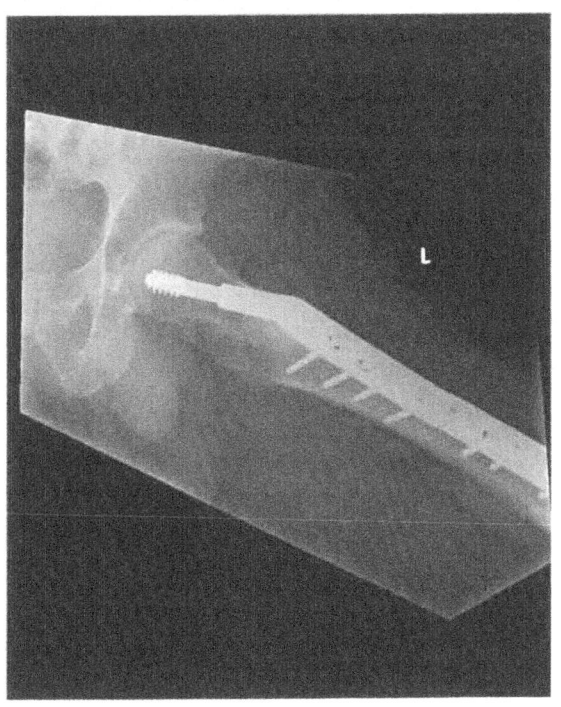

More medical and physiological assessments were in the pipeline, and it was suggested to me by my solicitor that it was important for my case that during the various phases of my recovery that I endeavour to try a college course or indeed return to work in some format. My sales director came out to the house one Monday morning to let me meet my colleagues, who were just delighted to see me alive. I sat through a meeting and presentation for about an hour, but it soon became clear to all concerned that there was no way back. My level of understanding, processing new information and memory loss all came to the fore like some massive tidal wave completely engulfing me. Next up was the computer course.

God, I struggled! Apart from being totally foreign to me in the first place, I found this so hard. I was having to relate to the manuals and instruction books for every single operation as my memory and learning abilities had just totally deserted me, and also gone was my power of concentration. Needless to say, things looked pretty bleak. By this time, it was now 1995, and there was still a lot of to-ing and fro-ing between the legal parties' concerns. Again, to try and put in my time, I decided to enrol in a sales and marketing course. This would be the perfect benchmark for me just to really test my progress, as this was completely my natural background, and by all rights, I should just sail through this. God! How wrong was I to be? Don't get me wrong; I enjoyed it immensely, as I could at least relate to some of it, but that was about as far as it went. Oh well, at least now on my new CV, I can use the phrase 'God loves a tryer'.

So, it is now the summer of 1996, three and a half years down the line, and I am absolutely gutted to hear my solicitor tell me that the figure my advocate has come up with is actually less than half of what my solicitor was sure the courts would offer me. I could not understand how there was to be such a massive discrepancy, and to be honest, my solicitor had no real answer for that either. However, this other traumatic episode ends with some miraculous news.

Fate surely had come to my rescue, as my solicitor informed me that the advocate involved has to be in London for some time, which has clashed with my Court of Session hearing date, and that the judge has requested that Scotland's top personal injury advocate be asked to take on my case. Wow! I cannot get my head around the size of the settlement amount he is quoting me. Totally night and day compared to the original advocate.

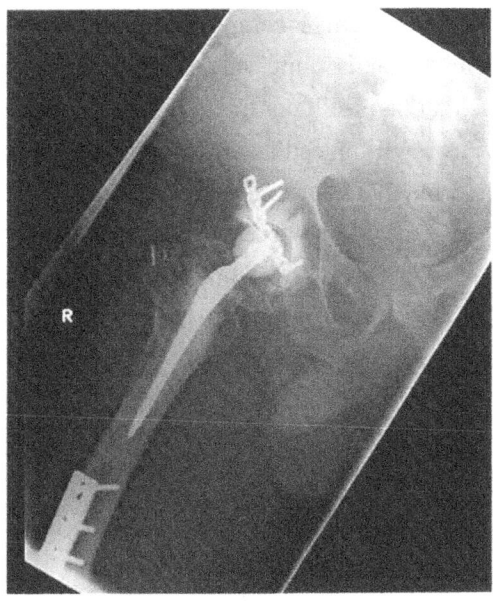

So now, here I am in the Court of Session on the morning of my case. I am asked to take a seat in the court's central lobby, where the floor tiles remind me of draught board, and in the meantime, my advocate and the defence advocate are strutting their stuff whilst facing up and down and around and around the 'draught board'. This seems like an endless procession of deliberation and negotiation with my future being the subject matter. At last, and after a few hours, my advocate comes to me and says that the defence is not prepared to settle out of court and that now my case will be heard next. We are asked to make our way into court, and just as the judge is about to take his chair, my advocate quickly asks for an adjournment, as at the very last minute an out-of-court offer is made and is put to me. My advocate informs me that it is a good and fair offer but that he feels he could get more, so he gives me fifteen minutes to think it over.

By this time, I am a complete shaking wreck, as the amount in question is quite staggering. On his return, he informs me that he is still confident that if we go back to the court, the judge will indeed award me more, but that there is no guarantee and that he may even award me less. So, on this latest advice, I decide to accept the out-of-court offer and thank him most sincerely for all his efforts. Wow! What a day, and what an end to three years of living and just surviving in a continuous state of limbo!

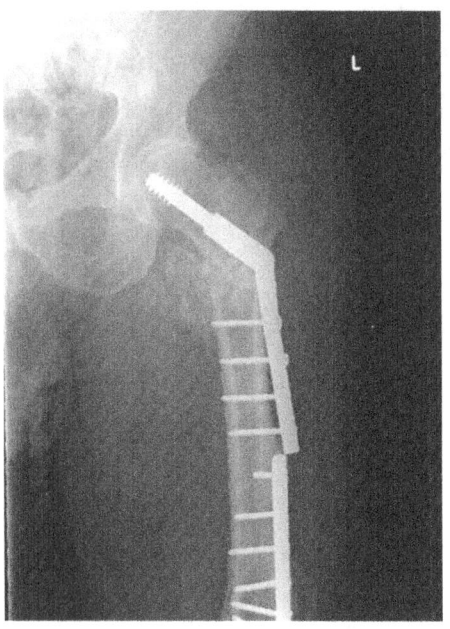

This request has come about as the Caravan social club are holding a charity fundraiser by way of a '70s and '80s music fancy dress-themed night. Well, excuse the pun, but this was music to my ears.

I am so in my element as my music HERO of all time was none other than the man, I call God…David Bowie, who amongst his music talent, his other claim to FAME was the fact that he had two different coloured eyes, so needless to say, I see this as a massive opportunity to try and replicate this and hopefully prove to be quite unique at the party.

I eventually contacted the ocular prosthetic technician to give him his Latin name, but to you and me… Glass Eye specialist.

I tell him my David Bowie story and that all the monies raised on the night will be donated to charity. He agrees to help me with this and says I can come to him whereby he will size the glass eye required to make a good fit, etc. This will in turn complement my natural brown eye.

This he duly does, and I am delighted. Two different coloured eyes! Wow! All I need now is for one of the Caravanners, who is a make-up artist to put the Aladdin Sane 'Zig Zag' on my face, together with black eyeliner and the purchase of an auburn wig and I'll be sorted.

What an entrance! What a night!

Chapter Six
Sailing the Seven Seas

"A tuxedo or a glamorous frock does not necessarily cover up the arsehole within."

This title is actually a quote from a first officer on one of the ships we sailed on and who became a very good friend. My god, the stories he could tell would be completely unbelievable if I had not actually witnessed them for myself.

What I am about to write in this final chapter is really just a snippet of the high and low lights compiled from our years of cruising.

Our first cruise very nearly ended in disaster, as we encountered a severe hurricane as we entered the Bay of Biscay after leaving Southampton just a few days earlier. At first, I started to think this experience was normal, and it was not until the second day of this that I realised this was far from normal when all the creaking started and lifeboat provisions were getting checked and about to be loaded onto pallets. Very scary indeed. This was confirmed officially by the captain of said ship when I met him a year later at a wedding reception where the two of us were, and this obviously became a topic of conversation.

So many ports and countries visited in all my years of cruising, but not wanting to make this chapter sound too boring, I have cherry-picked what I deem to range from quite unbelievable to extremely humorous behaviour by my fellow passengers. The restaurant tables were the most notorious place to meet and communicate with the passengers, and it was here that first impressions and opinions were born. I was much more at home and felt that I had more in common with the mix of crew than I ever did with the passengers, and this was typical of all my cruises. Most of the cabaret on the ship did not just happen in the theatre but could be witnessed all over the ship, so much so that some of the comedians who performed in the theatre actually used what they had endeavoured during their short time on the ship. One of the topical themes that they used was that of passengers fighting in the laundry rooms. This was known to be quite nasty at times, and many a bloody nose or worse was known to have happened. We were also to hear through the continuous gossip columns about two female passengers who were kicked off the ship in Cairns, Australia, for shoplifting. Would you believe it! One of the best laughs we had was the deputy captain's reply to the many passengers who asked how we would know when we were crossing the equator. His reply was to tell them that the ship's horn would sound, and if they went out onto the open decks at this point, then they would be able to see the faint red line in the sea that would denote the equator. My god! I have never seen so many cameras and binoculars pointing at thin air. Talk about being gullible! There was also a standing joke that there were actually two casinos on the ship, one being the actual casino and the other being the sick bay. This came about due to the scale of the medical fees they would charge for those who had the misfortune of falling ill. No wonder the British ships were registered in the Bahamas, etc. Just a typical money-making exercise so as to stop the British National Health Service free cover from coming into play should the ships be registered in the UK. They are not daft, you know!

One of our port excursions took us to Acapulco in Mexico, whereby we were to spend the day at a beach club resort, and very pleasant it was too. At the end of the day, before going on to the bus that was to take us back to the ship, I needed to go to the washroom. Upon entering the complex, I could not believe my eyes when the passenger from the ship was having a pee in the sink. As I was standing, having a pee in the proper place, another passenger who was standing next to me said, "Did you see that man taking a leak in one of the handwash basin?" I told him I did and said I was intrigued to find out why. The chap said to me that he would ask him and tell me his reason once we were back on the bus. Sure enough, he came up to me and said that after asking him why he peed in the basin, his arrogant reply was, 'because I can'. This was very strange, to say the least, but after much investigation when we were back on the ship, it turned out that he was a retired chief inspector with the London Metropolitan Police. Talk about abusing your position!

The next seeing is believing scenario was just in a couple of days' time, whereby the queue from the buffet lunch restaurant was so long out on to the deck you would have thought it was a conga dance in full swing. But, oh no! It was all down to the elderly couple. The man with his plate on his tray had his wife let him sample all that was on offer via her fork before he decided what he preferred and then put it on his plate. What a bloody nerve! Some folks have no shame. To cap it all and on the same subject, whilst using the elevator to return to my cabin, the said couple standing next to me were having a fully blown conversation discussing the thickness of the crust on their chosen bread. It just gets better!

Whilst relaxing in my cabin, the captain came over the PA and asked if there was any passenger with a certain blood type, as he was requesting they make their way to the sick bay due to the fact that a crewmember had seriously cut his hand and had lost a lot of blood. The good news is that enough blood was donated, and the crewmember recovered okay. However, what puzzled me was the fact that the request for blood was not also made to the crew.

After asking a senior officer about this, he told me to behave myself and said to me that I have obviously no idea what goes on regularly in the crew deck. He proceeded to inform me that they were all at it like rabbits and with different partners all the time, so the ship could absolutely never request that they donate blood. To try and justify this, I was told that nine months at sea was a very long time indeed. Yes, it sure is!

Another interesting and quite unbelievable situation I witnessed on one of the ships was that of the woman who brought four suitcases for herself. She and her husband had boarded the ship at Southampton, so there were no luggage restrictions as no flying was involved. After questioning her as to why she had so many cases, her reply was that she was not spending anytime on a cruise vacation by doing laundry. This resulted, can you believe it, in her donating four cases of dirty laundry to some of the crew, but they were informed they would need to wash all the contents first. What a snob, if ever I saw one!

Then there was an elderly Australian widow who was spending all her money on continually cruising the world. She informed us that she had sold her property together with all her substantial savings, and this was the way she chose to see out her final years. This was better than having her property taken from her in order to maintain any future stay in a residential home, etc. The ship became her residential home, and she informed us that there were only two ways she would leave this amazing existence, and that was either when the money ran out or in a box. What a way to go!

As it happened, I was approached on a couple of occasions, once by a member of the 'blue rinse brigade' who was looking for a husband and the other by a much younger female who was basically just looking for a quick tryst. Turned out that this woman, who was given the name 'she-devil', was a carer for an elderly gentleman in a wheelchair. The deal there was that she was free to do and spend what she wanted as long as she always returned to her cabin in order to tuck in her client. Take out of that what you will!

The cookery demonstration on board from the in-house executive chefs was something to be seen to be believed. After quite intensive and methodical demonstrations of all things delicious, it is time to sample the goodies on offer, but oh my God, the vultures waiting to swoop would be a massive understatement. Talk about wanting something for nothing, and the main guilty parties are the fur coats and no knickers brigade. Not an ounce of manners or morals to their name. Just as quick as they could stuff their faces and move on to the next free bay. Such sad individuals!

You do indeed witness everything on a cruise – warts and all.

Glossary

Shogun: Mitsubishi Shogun, make of a car
Sod: slang name for an indifferent person
Grouse: a polite name for a bitch
Fairy Liquid: a brand name for dish-washing liquid
Catweazle: 1980s British wrestler who was notorious for his unshaven, scruffy appearance
'Twinkle Toes': nickname of Heart's player Jimmy Wardhaugh because he could dance with a football
Jambo: a Heart's supporter
P.M.R.: Princess Margaret Rose, name of a hospital
'Bollocks': Scots name for nonsense
Pleurisy: proper medical name, so no need to define it
Hibs: short for Hibernian, a football club
Geordie: name of a person that comes from Newcastle
Larry: as happy as a person can be
Real McCoy: the absolute best
Maxi Boy: what we sometimes called our dog
Banshee: a person who screams and yells
Choppy: nickname for a man who is feeling good; a happy chappy
Limbo: left in limbo, indecisive, in between, etc.

Postscript

The knowledge and many of life's experiences that I have gained in the twenty-five years since my accident, together with the friendships, will remain with me forever.

As you will see in the book, however, I have witnessed a lot of the dark side of people from all walks of life from a behavioural point of view, which has led me to take a somewhat cynical view when writing various elements of the book.

I hope you will take out of it some of the experiences when perhaps you choose to plan on a similar journey and can now better prepare yourself that there will be many situations that you encounter that 'Not All Will Be As It Seems'!

Made in the USA
Monee, IL
03 May 2026

49437438R00036